PLAYING

RIGHT FIELD

PLAYING RIGHT FIELD

SCHOLASTIC INC.

New York

by **WillyWelch**

illustrated by
MarcSimont

Library of Congress Cataloging-in-Publication Data

Welch, Willy.
Playing right field / by Willy Welch; illustrated by Marc Simont.
p.   cm.
Summary: Although he is always chosen last and sent to play in right field, a young boy discovers the importance of that position.
ISBN 0-590-48298-X
1. Children's songs — Texts. [1. Baseball — Songs and music.
2. Songs.] I. Simont, Marc, ill. II. Title.
PZ8.3.W44P1   1995
[E] — dc20   94-18878
CIP
AC

12 11 10 9 8 7 6 5 4 3   5 6 7 8 9/9 0/0

Printed in the U.S.A.   37

First printing, April 1995

Marc Simont used charcoal and watercolors
to create the illustrations for this book.

Book design by Claire Counihan
and Marc Simont

To Wendy, Grady, and
Molly Bess
— W.W.

To the members of
the Cornwall Consolidated School
baseball team
— M.S.

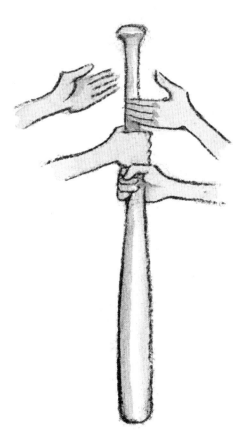

Saturday summers, when I was a kid,

we'd run to the school yard, and here's what we did.

We'd pick out the captains and choose up the teams.

It was always a measure of my self-esteem

because the strongest and fastest played shortstop and first.

The last ones they picked were the worst.

I never needed to ask. It was sealed.

I just took up my place in right field.

Playing right field, it's easy, you know.

You can be awkward and you can be slow.

That's why I'm here in right field

watching the dandelions grow.

Playing right field can be lonely and dull.

Little Leagues never have lefties that pull.

I'd dream of the day they'd hit one my way.
They never did. But still I would pray
that I'd make a fantastic catch on the run
and not lose the ball in the sun.

Then I'd awake from this long reverie
and pray that the ball never came out to me.

Sometimes I'd dream I was Mathews or Mays
hitting home runs and making great plays.

willie mays

Willie Mays

SAN FRANCISCO GIANTS
OUTFIELD

But they were so graceful, and they were so fast;

they never batted last.

Off in the distance, the game's dragging on.

There are strikes on the batter; some runners are on.

I don't know the inning. I've forgotten the score.

The whole team is yelling and I don't know what for.

Suddenly everyone's looking at me.

My mind has been wandering. What could it be?

They point to the sky and I look up above.

And a baseball falls into my glove!

Here in right field, it's important, you know.

You've got to know how to catch.

You've got to know how to throw.

That's why I'm here in right field

watching the dandelions grow.

SEP 2 6 1995

SEP 2 6 1995